W9-CAG-005

YOUR UNOFFICIAL GUIDE TO EVERYTHING SPICE

Photo Credits: p.1: A.P.R.F./Casper/Shooting Star pp.4-5: Alan Davidson/Retna; Guy Aroch/Retna pp.6-7: Mick Hutson/Retna; Retna pp. 8-9: Retna; Camera Press/Retna; Dave Hogan/Retna; Retna pp. 10-11: Bob Gordon/Star File; Retna; A.P.R.F./Gail/Shooting Star pp. 12-13: Dave Parker/Globe Photo pp. 14-15: A.P.R.F. /Casper/Shooting Star pp. 16-17: Gareth Davies/Retna pp. 18-19: A.P.R.F./Gail/Shooting Star; Dave Parker/Globe Photo; Clavel/A.P.R.F./Shooting Star pp. 20-21: Phil Loftus/Retna; Stills/Retna pp. 22-23: David Corio/Retna; Dave Hogan/Retna p. 24: Dave Hogan/Retna pp. 26-27:A.P.R.F./Gail/ Shooting Star; Mouillon/A.P.R.F./Shooting Star pp. 28-29: Casper/ A.P.R.F./Shooting Star; A.P.R.F./Gail/Shooting Star pp. 30-31: Casper/A.P.R.F./Shooting Star; Ron Davis/Shooting Star pp. 32-33: James McCauley/Retna p. 34: A.P.R.F./Andra/ Shooting Star pp. 36-37: Bob Gordon/Star File; Jeffrey Mayer/Star File pp. 38-39: Barry King/Shooting Star; V. Zuffante/Star File pp. 40-41: Barry King/Shooting Star; Paul Fenton/Shooting Star pp. 42-43: Alpha/Globe Photo; Bob Gordon/Star File; (CD) Images © 1998 Photodisc, Inc. pp. 44-45: Paul Smith/Retna; Alan Davidson/Retna pp.46-47: Alpha/Globe Photo; Guy Aroch/Retna p. 48: David Corio/Retna.
Back cover: A.P.R.F./Casper/Shooting Star.

Book Design: Paula Jo Smith

If you purchased this book without a cover, you should be aware that this book is stolen property. It was reported as "unsold and destroyed" to the publisher, and neither the author nor the publisher has received any payment for this "stripped book."

No part of this publication may be reproduced in whole or in part, or stored in a retrieval system, or transmitted in any form or by any means, electronic, mechanical, photocopying, recording, or otherwise, without permission of the publisher. For information regarding permission, write to Scholastic Inc., Attention: Permissions Department, 555 Broadway, New York, NY 10012.

ISBN: 0-439-04298-4

Copyright © 1998 Kidsbooks, Inc.
All rights reserved. Published by Scholastic Inc.

SCHOLASTIC and associated logos are trademarks and/or registered trademarks of Scholastic Inc.

12 11 10 9 8   9/9 0 1 2 3/0

Printed in the U.S.A.
First Scholastic printing, September 1998

YOUR UNOFFICIAL GUIDE TO EVERYTHING SPICE

by Alexandra E. Fischer

SCHOLASTIC INC.
New York Toronto London Auckland Sydney
Mexico City New Delhi Hong Kong

Table of CONTENTS

INTRODUCTION

The Spice Girls, as if you didn't already know, are a fabulous pop phenomenon that burst onto the music scene in July of 1996. Since that time, the whole world has learned that these fearless females are dedicated to nothing but music, fun, and Girl Power! Despite their amazing popularity, these fiery British girls, with the exception of Victoria, come from normal, middle-class households and have had to work hard like anyone else to pay for rent and food. Now they have sold over thirty million albums, and are reported to be among the top fifty highest paid celebrities in the world.

Perhaps their first great claim to fame was doing what no other group in British history has done before—sending each of their first four singles to the number one spot on the charts! Since then, the Spice Girls have conquered not only America, but also the entire world with their catchy lyrics and foot-stomping beats. They recently recorded a commercial for Pepsi and released their first feature film, *Spice World*, which in its opening weekend in the U.S. made more money than the industry had predicted.

These days, the Spice Girls have overcome yet one more hurdle. In June of 1998, Geri Halliwell announced that she was leaving the group. And although she's no longer an official Spice Girl, her inspiring spirit is still a strong presence. As one of the founding members of the band, Ginger Spice will always be a Spice Girl in our hearts.

So, in just a couple of short years, the Spice Girls have gone from nobodies to *Billboard* chart-toppers. They went from the concert stage to the silver screen. Then they went from five to four. But nothing will get in the way of the Spice Girls most awesome achievement: becoming the greatest pop phenom of the nineties!

COMING TOGETHER

So how did these hot young women from England gain their superstar status? The Spice Girls story began when the five answered an ad and were chosen out of hundreds auditioning for an all-girl band. Once the original "fab five" were brought together, they were moved into a house in a London suburb, and went through months of lessons. Lessons for dancing, lessons for singing solo, lessons for singing together...you get the picture. The house wasn't luxurious. Geri, the oldest, had her own room, but the two Mels shared, as did Victoria with Emma. The bills were paid, each girl had a small allowance, and sometimes they went into the city. But mostly they just worked hard. At first there were fights. Geri argued with Emma and Victoria, who went home for the weekends when Geri thought they should all be working. But the girls soon became close friends, and at the end of their training they emerged strong, loud, proud, and flashy—and there's been no stopping them since.

So who are the darling divas who won pop stardom so quickly? They claim they are just "normal girls from England," while their fans know they're anything but normal!

VICTORIA ADDAMS is known as the "straightest" of all the Spice Girls. The other Spices say she's elegant, ladylike, and organized. But Posh says there's another side to her—she's a lot funnier than people think! She says, "Everyone seems to think...I don't ever speak and I've got no personality whatsoever, but...I've got a very dry sense of humor."

Victoria comes from a wealthy family, hence the nickname Posh. In fact, her father used to take her to school in a Rolls-Royce! Because she was well-off and shy, Victoria was unpopular and picked on by the other kids at school. But when she went on to a school to study dance, everything changed for her. She made good friends, and when she graduated, she started to audition for

VICTORIA ADDAMS
(POSH SPICE)

theater and dance troupes. Then she answered the ad for an all-girl band, and the rest is history.

Victoria loves to dress up and wear designer clothes, but she says she's the same person she always was before she made it big. The differences in her life that she notices are things like having the money to shop anywhere in the world, having someone straighten her hair rather than doing it herself, or owning 25 pairs of Gucci shoes instead of one.

MELANIE JANINE BROWN is the loudest of the bunch. (And that's saying a lot!) It seems she was always loud—she claims her mom used to send her to her aunt's house when she became too much to handle. And although her parents allowed her to take acting and ballet, Mel decided that wasn't enough for her. She tried out for and got into a school for performing arts.

When she left school, Mel, like the other Spices, hit the audition scene in between working other jobs such as telemarketing for a newspaper. Scary Spice says she loves to go clubbing and to shock people by doing crazy things. She's spontaneous

Pitt at a party, the other four were starstruck. Not Mel! She just walked up, slapped him on the back, and started talking to him.

But Scary Spice also has a very quiet, spiritual side. In fact, she writes poetry about her life. Mel B says you should always express your opinion and loves being in a band where you can do anything.

MELANIE JANINE BROWN (SCARY SPICE)

and outrageous and wants someday to own a "monster motorbike." Mel B is known for her willingness to play jokes and have a good time, maybe even more than the others, and she doesn't let anything stand in her way. For example, when the Spice Girls saw Brad

MELANIE JAYNE CHISHOLM is the most musically talented Spice Girl—according to many people. She's also known as the peacemaker of the group. When there are fights, Mel C is the one who listens to both sides of the argument and calms everyone down. The other Spice Girls appreciate this side of Mel C, but say it can be, "annoying if you want her to stick up for you." Mel C says she can also be irritating because she's "Little Miss Professional Head" when the Spice Girls are working, and that she's always trying to get the others to stop messing around.

However, as it turns out Mel C wasn't able to fix all the Spice Girls' arguments. It is believed that one of the reasons Geri may have left was because of the continuous fights she had with Mel B.

Mel is the one known for her tumbling onstage and in videos. She always has to be doing something athletic. She says the last thing she does before going to bed is fifty stomach crunches. No wonder she's in such great shape!

Mel C is disciplined in other parts of her life as well. She claims all the cans in her cupboards have to be facing one direction, and Geri has said all her clothes are folded neatly the same way.

When Mel is at home, she likes to watch soccer and cooking shows on TV, or she might go out to clubs with friends. And while she may not be in the spotlight as much as some of the other Spices, Mel says she's happy about that. "I'm the one the paparazzi don't follow. Touch wood [knock on wood]."

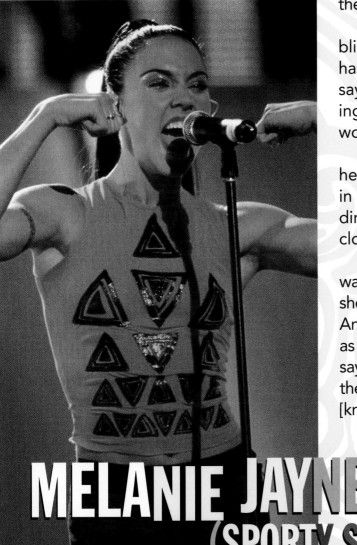

MELANIE JAYNE CHISHOLM
(SPORTY SPICE)

9

EMMA LEE BUNTON is the youngest of the group. And she says the others "have taught her a lot about growing up." She's affectionate and loves to cuddle, and her best friend is still her mom. "We're like best buddies," she says. "I really miss her when I go away." So at the end of 1996, when the Spices had some time off, she took her mom on vacation to the Caribbean island of Barbados.

Emma has been onstage since she entered a beauty contest at age three. Soon after that, she started modeling and making commercials, and she's never been out of the limelight since. The others say Emma is fun to hang out with, but they also say that they often get the blame for her pranks! And her tricks began way before she joined the band. Once, in school, Emma clogged all the drains with toilet paper and left the faucets running!

About being famous, Emma says, "I can be a real brat sometimes," but she doesn't let her ego get the best of her. "My mum taught me to be polite to people even if they weren't nice to you…." she says. Emma is happy to be able to "…show girls that if we can make it, so can they!"

EMMA LEE BUNTON
(BABY SPICE)

SPICE Girl
(July 1996-June 1998)

GERALDINE ESTELLE HALLIWELL, the oldest of the Spice Girls, is a "take charge" kind of person. She claims she's had to be, since she was the smallest of a large family, and always had to shout louder than the others to be heard.

When the girls first got together, Geri was the one who bullied everyone to work harder. She was so driven that she spent hours just practicing on her own. She also has a bit of a reckless streak—she once had a car that she crashed sev-

GERALDINE ESTELLE HALLIWELL
(GINGER SPICE)

en times in six months. And she tends to be forgetful; she's apparently terrible with names. But her bandmates say that Geri is the one who sees "the big picture" and is always planning ahead. The other Spices say that Geri is always saying, "This is what we're going to do…." And Geri herself says the last thing she does before going to bed is to "plan the next day."

Geri lived in Spain and in Turkey and had all kinds of jobs before she was a Spice Girl. She was a dancer, a cleaning person, and a presenter on television. So now that she's famous, Geri enjoys being able to send positive messages. She says, "It's so important for young kids to think, 'Hold on a minute, I can be an astronaut or a scientist if I want.'"

11

WHY THE SPICES

Okay, so we already know that the Spice Girls are the hottest band ever! But what made these beauteous Brits succeed where so many others have failed? GIRL POWER!!! Well, yes, but there are other reasons, too. Most important, instead of being totally unreachable megastars, they are just regular girls—even now. They don't dress in expensive clothes (except, of course, for Victoria), or insist on eating expensive food; they don't want to be worshipped; they just want to be real.

If there's one thing the Spice Girls are, it's honest. Emma says, "With us, what you see is what you get." They're not perfect and they know it. Geri always said, "We're proof that you don't have to be classically beautiful or six feet tall to be considered attractive...."

And Mel C agrees. "We're not beautiful. That's something we're proud of. We're five normal girls from England...." And that's a message the Spice Girls carry around the world. It's Girl Power. It's about being yourself, even if that means showing your faults. And chances are, there's a Spice Girl like you! Whether you're tall, small, quiet, loud, athletic, delicate, or somewhere in between, the Spices say that you're spicy, too!

12

ARE THE NICEST

The Spice Girls also know what their fans really, really want. Emma says, "Kids don't want to hear about wishy-washy love. We're talking about positive messages." The Spices say friendship, and being there for the people you care about, are more important than romance.

But almost as important is...having fun! The Spice Girls are wild, funny, goofy...outrageous! They love to make trouble wherever they go. And when they fall, they get back up again. For instance, Baby Spice seriously considered giving up her trademark platform boots when she twisted her ankle onstage. And Ginger Spice once got a fake fingernail stuck in her ear and had to have it removed! They make mistakes, just like everybody else—and they laugh about them.

And the recent news declaring Geri's departure from the Spice Girls tells us one more thing about them—being true to themselves is their first priority. This may have been the end of the five Spice Girls as we knew them. But it was a new beginning for Scary, Sporty, Baby, Posh, and Ginger.

So...the Spice Girls have made it clear who and what they really, really are, what they're really, really not, and most of all, what they really, really want! Who can argue with that?

13

The SPICE GIRLS on... the SPICE GIRLS!

Mel C says when she met the other Spice Girls: "Victoria is really, really lovely, but she's not as ladylike as she'd have everybody believe....But she's really a great mate [friend] and a good shoulder to cry on...."

"Me and Mel B compete to see who's the toughest—we're like the Gallagher brothers."

"...Mel B thinks I'm funny. We stick up for each other because we're both from up North."

Geri said: "If you want to chill out, Emma's voice is really soothing....If you want to get down, Mel C and Mel B can really belt it out and Victoria is amazing live."

"Emma might portray herself as being the sweet and innocent Spice, but it's not true. Me and Mel B always get the blame for her pranks."

We know what everyone says about the SPICES, but what do they say about each other?

Victoria says: "I thought Mel C was genuinely nice, and Geri was mad. I'd never met anyone who dressed like that before!...and I thought Mel B was really pretty."

"Emma is the loveliest, craziest, funniest girl to have around."

"Mel B is the ultimate Spice Girl—pretty, clever, crazy, and impudent. Sometimes I would like to be like she is."

Emma says: Mel B is "terrible in the mornings, and a total hypochondriac as well."

Mel C is "...a very funny person when you talk to her, and when she's got something to say, it's very important. And she gets us up and going when we've been a bit lazy....She's a cool chick."

"Victoria thinks about the consequences of things."

Mel B is "...the best person to go partying with. She won't just go to one club, she'll go to all of them."

Mel B says: "The best thing about being a Spice Girl is sticking with my mates and being able to shout loud and proud."

"Me and Mel C usually [pillow] fight a lot. But we're too tired these days." And Mel C says: "I usually win."

Emma "...gets away with murder. She's like one of those children who's really naughty and then gives you a kiss."

15

QUIZ: DO YOU HAVE

Do you do what you really, really want? Are you loyal to your friends? Take this quiz and find out just how spicy you are!

❶ The day before the sleep-over you and your friends have been planning for weeks, the boy you like calls to ask you to a movie—for the very same night! **You:**

a) Ditch your friends and go to the movie; your friends will understand.

b) Beg your friends to find dates and go to the movie with you.

c) Tell the boy you'd love to go with him, but ask to do it another night.

❷ You go shopping with some girls from class. They're all buying short skirts and tell you that you should, too. But you don't really like them. **You decide to:**

a) Buy the skirt and wear it. You want them to think you're cool.

b) Buy the skirt but hide it in your closet. Maybe they'll forget you were with them.

c) Pick a pair of jeans you've been looking at instead. They make you feel more like yourself.

❸ Your best friend just had a fight with her boyfriend. You've both been invited to go to a party that afternoon, but your friend doesn't want to go—she says she's too depressed. **You would:**

a) Go to the party and have fun. You'll spend some time with your friend later.

b) Insist that your friend come with you to the party. She shouldn't mope, after all, and that way you can enjoy yourself, too.

c) Stay with your friend and do stuff to cheer her up—there will be other parties, but your friend needs you now.

GIRL POWER?

4 You desperately want the starring role in the school musical, but you're afraid you aren't good enough or brave enough to get it. You have a month before the auditions. **You decide to:**

a) Not try out this year. Better not embarrass yourself in front of everyone.

b) Go to the auditions, but only ask for a part in the chorus.

c) Go for it! After all, what do you have to lose? You might mess up the audition, but at least you will have tried.

5 You tried out for the cheerleading squad, but you didn't make it. Those girls must have been practicing for months, and you had no idea it would be so competitive! You still want to be on the squad, **so you:**

a) Give up—you'll never make it out of all those people.

b) Wait until the next tryouts and give it another shot.

c) Start practicing now. By the time the next tryouts come around, you're going to be so good, there's no way they won't take you.

6 You're walking down the hall at school with a friend when you suddenly trip and go flying, dropping everything you're carrying. **You:**

a) Get up and run to the bathroom as fast as you can and hide there.

b) Blush, gather your stuff together, and head for your next class without taking your eyes off the floor.

c) Laugh at your clumsiness, gather up your stuff, and keep talking with your friend.

Answers:

Give yourself two points for every "c" answer, one point for every "b" answer, and 0 for "a" answers. **If you scored:**

9–12 You're so spicy, you're on fire!

5–8 You're getting there, but you need a little spicing up.

0–4 For now, you'll have to be content to be a wannabe. Lighten up and have some fun!

17

Six Reasons We Love The SPICE Girls

Emma:

❶ She can sing all the high parts.

❷ She's a great cuddler.

❸ She talked someone with a private plane into giving her a ride home from Portugal, just so she could see her mom.

❹ She loves eating pizza.

❺ She has a blue belt in Goju (a type of martial arts).

❻ She gets goose bumps when she hears a Spice Girls song.

Five Ways to SPICE Up Your Life

❶ Believe in yourself.

❷ Follow your dreams.

❸ Take control of your life.

❹ Admit your flaws.

❺ Be outrageous.

Mel B:

❶ The first thing she did when the Spice Girls made it big was buy her mom a car.

❷ She brought her cat to the set of the movie *Spice World*.

❸ She talks to her tropical fish.

❹ She sponsors a little African boy.

❺ She signs her name with a peace sign.

❻ She still wears glasses.

(Former Spice Girl) Geri:

❶ She thinks the best thing about being famous is making a difference in the world.

❷ She says she would like to have been Mother Teresa.

❸ She admits she's bad at expressing her feelings.

❹ She once gave a fan something from her own wardrobe.

❺ She cries at sad movies.

❻ She says she'll be back….

Mel C:

❶ She loves singing even though she doesn't think she's a great singer.

❷ **She loves to go grocery shopping.**

❸ She believes you should never be judged by your clothes.

❹ **She says she'll do anything onstage.**

❺ She cried when the Spices turned on the London Christmas lights.

❻ **She always goes jogging, even when she's on tour.**

Victoria:

❶ She was once pulled over because the police thought she was too young to be driving such a fancy car.

❷ **She admits to being shy.**

❸ She says if she were an animal, she'd be a cat.

❹ **When she was in school, she did all her homework and got good grades.**

❺ When she was living with the band, she went home every weekend to be with her family.

❻ **She always knew she wanted to be famous.**

We all know the Spices by the nicknames they earned when they first started out. But we've found out a lot more about them since then. Do you still think their nicknames suit them? Maybe you could come up with better ones. For example, Mel B is proud of being loud, so maybe she could be Noisy Spice. And Geri claims she was always telling the others what to do, so she could have been Bossy Spice. Create your own nicknames for your favorite five.

Mel B:

_____

Emma:

_____

Geri (Former Spice Girl)**:**

_____

Mel C:

_____

Victoria:

_____

Everyone knows the Spice Girls are busy women. But what actually goes on when they are working? Here are some examples of what their hectic days are like.

ALLWORK and NO PLAY?

On a recent trip to Madrid, Spain, the girls' schedules looked something like this:

7:30 a.m. (London time)—plane leaves London airport.

11:00 a.m. (Spain time)—girls arrive at the Madrid airport, get in car and are driven into the city.

1:00 p.m.—after a half hour of trying to get past fans, enter radio station.

1:30–4:30 p.m.—group interview with journalists, photographers, and reporters, and a visit with fan club members.

5:00–6:30 p.m.—makeup, hair, and wardrobe changes.

7:00 p.m.—free public performance for over 20,000 people.

9:00 p.m.—live appearance on a radio show.

At home in London, a day of publicity is not much easier:

10:00 a.m.—arrive at the photo studio.

10:30–11:30 a.m.—makeup, hair, and wardrobe.

12:00 p.m.—photo shoot for the cover of a British soccer magazine.

1:00 p.m.—off to another studio where makeup, hair, and wardrobe are changed for a photo shoot for a British celebrity magazine. While the girls are having their makeup and hair done, a reporter interviews them.

2:00 p.m.—photo shoot.

3:00 p.m.—leave for another studio where they change clothes, makeup, and hair again for a fashion magazine shoot.

9:00 p.m.—finished for the day.

Victoria answers questions from millions of cyber-fans online.

The girls are free to go home, go out, see friends, or just go to bed, which is what they decide to do.

The day after this grueling schedule, the girls get a much-needed break. But the day after that, they head off to Lapland for two days with 50 MTV contest winners and 150 journalists from all over the world. The day after that, the girls have to be back in London to pick the lottery numbers.

An evening with the Spice Girls in the Big Apple:

The Spices have all been fighting the flu, but they board a tour bus with twenty local radio contest winners.

First stop: a fancy restaurant for appetizers.

Second stop: Great American Backrub for head massages.

Third stop: another wild restaurant for dinner.

And in between: live interviews with the radio station over a cell phone, an interview with a reporter from a celebrity magazine, giving advice and talking to fans, singing and dancing to Spice music.

Another night, they will pose in the freezing wind atop the Empire State Building for a photographer who is hanging out of a helicopter.

Sound glamorous? Maybe not, but still, the girls make the best of it. Mel C says, "Even though we're really tired...I truly believe that we are the luckiest five girls on earth. I know that sounds eurghhhh, but I do."

THE REAL SPICE SCOOP

Can you separate the fact from fiction in the Spice Girls story? Answer true or false to each of these facts or faux and find out.

1 The original Spice management wanted the band to have one lead singer and make the rest of the girls backup.

True_____ False_____

2 Originally, the band was going to be called "Silk."

True_____ False_____

3 All five of the Spice Girls answered an advertisement for a girl band in a newspaper called *The Stage*.

True_____ False_____

4 The Spice Girls' first management told each girl how to dress.

True_____ False_____

5 Emma was the first girl offered the chance to replace Michelle Stephenson.

True_____ False_____

6 All the girls had been professional singers before they formed the band.

True_____ False_____

7 Mel C and Mel B were roommates even before the band got together.

True_____ False__

8 The Spice Girls put on a live performance in order to get an agent to sign them.

True_____ False_____

Answers:

1. True 2. False, it was going to be called "Touch." 3. False, only four of the five Spice Girls answered the ad. Emma joined the group later. 4. False. The girls have always dressed the way they do now. 5. False, she was the second; Abigail Kis was the first. 6. False, all of the girls needed training, although some had sung before. 7. False, the girls met for the first time when the band was formed. 8. True

23

A SPICY Alphabet

A
Adventurous
Always look for new challenges.

B
Boldness
Never be afraid to speak your mind.

C
Charisma
The Spice Girls really know how to turn it on!

D
Diva
Self-confidence is the best medicine!

E
Enthusiasm
Do everything 100%.

F
Friendship
Girls know what's really important.

G
Girl Power
Girls should stick together.

H
Harmony
The Spices believe in it!

I
Independence
Do what you believe is right!

J
Jazzy
Do everything with style and flair.

K
Kinetic
The Spice Girls are in constant motion!

L
Loyalty
Be true to yourself and your beliefs.

M
Music
That's what it's all about!

N
Noisy
Be proud to be loud.

O
Outrageous
The Spices always have a good time.

P
Powerful
Take control of your life and make your own decisions.

Q
Quintet
Whether they're five or four, the Spices are still number one!

R
Real
Be yourself!

S
Style
The Spices know what's hot.

T
Tenacious
Never give up your dreams.

U
Unity
With good friends, "you'll never walk alone."

V
Verve
Spicy girls have spunk and style.

W
Wit
If you fall, laugh it off!

X
X-tra
Work extra hard to achieve your goals.

Y
Yell
Be heard, even if you have to shout.

Z
Zigazig ha
Be creative and get what you really, really want!

SPICE SPLASH

EMMA
aka Baby Spice:

Full Name: Emma Lee Bunton

Born: January 21, 1976, in Finchley, North London

Sign: Aquarius

Hair: Blond

Eyes: Blue

Height: 5'2"

Distinguishing Marks: None

Loves: Her mom, cuddling, doughnuts

Hates: Macho men

Fears: Loneliness

Motto: "Be sweet, be good, and honest—always."

Not-So-Secret Crush: George Clooney

Favorite Song to Perform Live: "2 Become 1"

Favorite Word: Candyfloss

Favorite Movies: *Pollyanna, Toy Story*

SPICE SPLASH

(Former Spice Girl) GERI aka Ginger Spice:

Full Name: Geraldine Estelle Halliwell

Born: August 8, 1972, in Watford, England

Sign: Leo

Hair: Red

Eyes: Blue

Height: 5'2"

Distinguishing Marks: Pierced bellybutton, tattoo on lower back

Loves: Old movies, dressing up

Hates: Men with big egos

Describes herself as: "Eccentric, inquisitive, psycho, friendly, and loving."

Motto: "She who dares, wins."

Not-So-Secret Crush: Bryan Adams

First Record Ever Bought: "Dancing Queen" by Abba

First Live Concert Attended: Wham!

Favorite Song to Perform Live: "Denying"

Favorite Word: Existentialism

MEL B
aka Scary Spice:

Full Name: Melanie Janine Brown

Born: May 29, 1975, in Leeds, England

Sign: Gemini

Hair: Brown

Eyes: Brown

Height: 5'5"

Distinguishing Marks: Pierced tongue, tattoo on stomach

Loves: Fish and chips, shocking people

Hates: Salads, weak men

Fears: Spiders

Not-So-Secret Crush: George Clooney

First Record Ever Bought: "Mickey" by Toni Basil

First Live Concert Attended: Janet Jackson

Favorite Song to Perform Live: "Do It"

Favorite Words: Higgledy-piggledy, hotch-potch

Favorite Movie: *Pulp Fiction*

SPICE SPLASH

MEL C
aka Sporty Spice:

Full Name: Melanie Jayne Chisholm

Born: January 12, 1974, in Widnes, England

Sign: Capricorn

Hair: Brown

Eyes: Hazel

Height: 5'6"

Distinguishing Marks: Pierced nose and two tattoos — both on her right arm

Loves: Chinese food, soccer

Hates: Smoking, rude people, lazy men

Describes herself as: Shy when she meets people

Not-So-Secret Crush: Soccer player Jamie Redknapp, Bruce Willis

Favorite Song to Perform Live: "…That's a tough one because they're all so different…."

Favorite Song: "Song 2" by Blur

Favorite Movie: *Toy Story*

Favorite Artist: Stevie Wonder

SPICE SPLASH

VICTORIA
aka Posh Spice:

Full Name: Victoria Addams

Born: April 7, 1975, in Hertfordshire, England

Sign: Aries

Hair: Brown

Eyes: Brown

Height: 5'6"

Distinguishing Marks:
Pierced fingernail

Loves: Sappy movies, designer clothes

Hates: Japanese food, being called "Vicky," men with bad shoes

Describes Herself As: A worrier, funny, and impatient

Not-So-Secret Crush: Ray Liotta, and her fiancé, David Beckham

Favorite Song to Perform Live:
"If You Can't Dance"

Favorite Artists: Anita Baker, Toni Braxton, Barbra Streisand

Least Favorite Song: "Love Shack" by the B-52s

SPICE Boys?

The Spice Girls are known to be firm in their stance on where men fit into their lives. For example, Emma once said that Mel B is very useful because "If you get into an awkward situation with a boy, she'll rescue you by pointing at him and shouting, 'No!'" Understandably, most men would be scared of Scary and the other Spices. So the question really is, *do* men fit into their very busy lives?

The answer is yes, at least for one very engaged Posh Spice, who is set to marry British soccer star David Beckham in May of next year. Are the other Spices invited? What a question! The other girls were asked to be maids of honor.

Mel B broke up with Icelander Fjolnir Thorjeirsson in March after a year-long romance. She was soon dating backup dancer on the *Spice World* tour, Jimmy Gulzar. And in mid-May, a newspaper reported that the two were engaged at a Paris restaurant during a break from the tour. So it looks as though two of the Spices are serious!

The other girls have had their share of romance in the past few years as well. Geri was dating another backup *Spice World* tour dancer. Emma dated someone outside of showbiz, dental technician Mark Vergueze for quite a while, and she said, "I love it when I go home because...he just relates to me. When we get together we don't even talk about the group." Mel C agrees with Emma about the kind of guys she likes to date. For example, Mel C says her career definitely comes first, but when she has a boyfriend, she doesn't want one who's a pop star as well.

So the answer to the Spice Boys question seems to be that, yes, the Spice Girls do have time for the men in their lives. But like everything else, they have strong opinions about where they fit in.

How much do you really know about the Spice Girls and Geri?
Fill in the blank with the name of the Spice who fits and find
out. Match your answers with those at the bottom of the page.

QUIZ! TEST YOUR SPICE QUOTIENT

1 _____ once said, "I don't do quiet!"

2 _____ hates the way she looks when she smiles.

3 _____ is Prince William's favorite Spice Girl.

4 _____ once worked as an aerobics instructor.

5 _____ thinks one of her main talents is walking in high heels.

6 _____ has a large collection of smelly soaps.

7 _____'s favorite expression is, "This is what we're going to do...."

8 _____ once auditioned for the musical *Cats*.

9 _____ only played with boys growing up because, "Girls were always crybabies."

10 _____ claims, "I've never in my life succeeded in reading a book from cover to cover!"

32

⑪ _____ once took voice lessons from the woman who later was the Spice Girls' vocal coach.

⑫ _____ likes her apartment to be clean, but hates anything to do with housework.

⑬ _____ used to have Madonna parties, where everyone would dress and act like Madonna.

⑭ _____ says she doesn't really get presents from fans like the other Spices.

⑮ _____, _____, and _____ have tattoos.

⑯ _____ admits she used to pick gum up off floors.

⑰ _____ says she's shy when she meets people, but not onstage.

Answers:

1. Mel B 2. Victoria 3. Emma 4. Geri 5. Victoria 6. Emma 7. Geri 8. Mel C 9. Mel B 10. Victoria 11. Emma 12. Mel C 13. Emma 14. Victoria 15. Geri, Mel C, and Mel B 16. Mel B 17. Mel C

The SPICE GIRLS Speak!

The SPICE Girls have a lot to say, so let's hear it!

What Is Girl Power?

"It's about equality and having fun and trying to run your life." —Mel B

"It means a lot of things. To me, it means accepting yourself, learning to love yourself, and being a strong female. And not taking any rubbish from men." —Mel C

"For me, Girl Power is respecting yourself as well as others." —Emma

"It's looking at yourself in the mirror and saying, 'This is me, I'm going to make the best of it. I'm going to have fun, I'm going to have a positive attitude. I'm not going to be dominated by anyone." —Victoria

The SPICE Girls

"I think we're not role models, but we do have a responsibility and enjoy giving positivity and fun!" —Emma

"You can get away with anything as long as you're cheeky." —Mel B

"Do I think Margaret Thatcher is the original Spice Girl? Not particularly. My mum is." —Emma

"We have been through so many bad times together, so many highs together, you can't express how that makes you be with someone."
—Mel B

The Best Thing About Being Famous Is...

"...meeting fans and being able to have music released." —Mel C

"Everything is the best. Even if it's negative, we turn it into a positive."
—Emma

The Worst Thing About Being Famous Is...

"We're all knackered [exhausted]. For over a year we've been working nonstop, flying here and there. It's relentless. We've been doing fourteen-hour days for months. Underneath all this makeup, I've got black 'round my eyes." —Victoria

"I know it sounds ungrateful, but sometimes fame isn't that much fun. You're visiting all these fantastic places and you'll be sitting there moaning, 'I want to go home.'" —Mel C

Are Boys Important?

"Boyfriends should never rule your life or come between you and your friends."—Mel B

"Friendship is better than a boyfriend...because it will last forever."—Mel C

"At the moment my career is my priority, but...I want to have un-popstar boyfriends."—Mel C

What Do You Like About Yourself?

"I like to think my talent is giving every person I come in contact with a bit of zest for life again."—Mel B

"I'm very determined. I think I can be a bit annoying, but I'm glad I'm like that. I don't think I'm a great singer, but I love it."—Mel C

"I think I can talk to anybody, and I always try to understand people."—Geri

On the Road With the SPICE Girls

What's it really like to be a Spice Girl, up on the stage with all those adoring fans screaming for you?

Whether they're on the road or at home in England, the hottest girl band ever is always up for fun. But do they get tired of endless hotel rooms around the world? No! The Spices say one of the best things about traveling so much is being able to meet other celebs from all over. Baby Spice claims she still gets starstruck, even though she's a megastar herself.

But what else do they do besides perform and meet other superstars? Well, true to their spicy natures, Sporty tries to eat properly and work out when she has spare time (spare time? what spare time?), while Victoria goes shopping, of course. In fact, they all agree that shopping is one of their favorite things to do. There are things the girls do not leave home without. For example, Emma always brings her hair elastics for true Baby beauty. Victoria brings her hair straighteners. And Mel C? You guessed it—running shoes!

Before every appearance and performance, the Spice Girls sit through hours of makeup and hairstyling. Finally, they dress and are ready to go on. Do they have any rituals? Emma says, "...we'd hype ourselves up by marching and punching the air." And in the end, it's all worth it.

According to Mel C, there's nothing like performing live. She says, "Getting up on stage is the best feeling in the world—it's what the Spice Girls are all about." And the fans obviously think it's worth it, too.

And even though Geri is officially no longer a Spice Girl, she will never lose her love for being onstage. "It's complete emancipation, liberation, and freedom. It's gratifying receiving that warm adoration...."

With a passion that burns this strong for music, perhaps one day we can see a Spice reunion.

37

SPICE WORLD
The MOVIE

After their debut album, *SPICE*, zoomed to number one all over the world, the Spice Girls decided that megamusic stardom just wasn't enough. So, they made a movie! *Spice World* was released in late 1997 in England, early 1998 in the U.S., and Spice fans turned out in force to see this witty, wacky celebration of everything Spice.

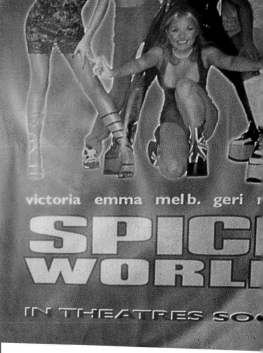

victoria emma mel b. geri

SPICE
WORLD

IN THEATRES SO

The plot (if there really is one) revolves around a week in the life of an amazingly successful band preparing for its first ever live show. It follows the band through all of the wild and wonderful things that happen to them along the way.

The Conflicts:

- The Spice Girls' manager is trying to control everything they do (very unspicy!) while the girls are just trying to have some fun!

- A newspaper editor out to ruin their careers tells a photographer to follow them and try to pick up anti-Spice vibes.

- A weird filmmaker is also following them around.

- A Hollywood producer is trying to convince them to star in a film he has no story for!

- Their best friend has asked them to be god-mothers to her baby, which is about to be born.

Sound confusing?? Well...the lives of the fabulous five are nothing if not hectic. The movie is really about the Spice Girls, of course—five

39

young pop stars trying to have a good time in the midst of the craziness that is their life. And the making of the movie was a definite part of that madness. The cast and crew had only 43 days to film. And every day they were surrounded by security guards, screaming fans, and photographers. In fact, the media was working hard to earn the teasing they get in the movie—hanging out of windows, following members of the crew, dressing up as construction workers, and hiding in the bushes! It was a crazy time, but everyone had fun thanks to the Spices' energy and enthusiasm.

Kim Fuller, one of the screenwriters, said, "The people who've been involved so far... have loved it....Energy permeates the whole process of the film."

All five of the girls seem to agree on which were their favorite scenes to shoot. The Spices liked when they could just "banter with each other," and let their "imaginations run wild." They all loved the live performance shots. And they all agree that it was cool to dress up as the Spice Girl most unlike them. (Victoria was Emma, Emma was Mel B, Mel B was Geri, Geri was Mel C, and Mel C was Victoria.) Emma said, "It was really cool dressing up as each other. I thought Victoria looked great as me—much better than me, in fact!" And Mel C thought, "Trying to be Victoria was a bit of a nightmare....I thought I was going to break her dainty little shoes...."

SPICE WORLD
Behind the Scenes

Did the Spice Girls like everything about making the movie?

Well…no. Mel C and Victoria had to spend a whole day of filming getting in and out of freezing cold water. And Victoria said that wearing the same clothes over

and over again got to be a drag. But probably the toughest thing about filming the movie was the early mornings and late nights. The Spice Girls said they were too tired to do much of anything except work and sleep.

In fact, here's an example of a day's schedule on the movie set:

6 a.m.—picked up and driven to the location.

6:30–9:30 a.m.—makeup, hair, and wardrobe.

9:30 a.m.–12:30 p.m.—sitting in the cabin of a boat waiting to begin filming—and feeling very seasick!

1:00 p.m.—filming finally begins, and involves Victoria and Mel C falling into the water. Since everyone keeps getting the timing wrong, they have to film it over and over and over again.

6:30 p.m.—finished filming for the day.

7:30 p.m.—into the portable studio to work on the album. Album? That's right! The Spice Girls recorded the new album at the same time they were filming the movie.

What did the Spices do with those spare moments when they weren't filming but had to be near the set? There was always something to occupy them, from signing autographs to shopping, to watching television. There was even time to just hang out, eat, and talk in the trailers. Victoria said, "We had a laugh on the set like we always do, wherever we are."

DISCO

SPICE

Released in 1996 by Virgin Records

1. Wannabe	2:52
2. Say You'll Be There	3:56
3. 2 Become 1	4:00
4. Love Thing	3:37
5. Last Time Lover	3:37
6. Mama	5:03
7. Who Do You Think You Are	3:59
8. Something Kinda Funny	4:02
9. If You Can't Dance	3:58

GRAPHY

SPICE WORLD

Released in November 1997
by Virgin Records

1. Spice Up Your Life	2:53
2. Stop	3:24
3. Too Much	4:31
4. Saturday Night Divas	4:25
5. Never Give Up the Good Times	4:30
6. Move Over	2:46
7. Do It	4:04
8. Denying	3:46
9. Viva Forever	5:09
10. Lady Is a Vamp	3:09

And the Winner Is...

It seems that the Spice Girls have done just about everything—commercials, movies, albums, videos. In Britain, they even have their own deodorants. And it seems as if this success has come almost overnight for the sultry superstars. We, as true Spice fans, know that their fame came only after hard work, practice, and sheer willpower. But along the way, the fab five have managed to pick up some awards.

Their first award show was the 1997 Brit Awards, which are equal to America's Grammy Awards. And that first year, the Spice Girls nabbed two of the most important awards: Best British Single, for "Wannabe," and Best British Video, for "Say You'll Be There." At the 1997 World Music Awards they picked up the bid for Best Newcomer.

Their next big showing was at the 1997 MTV European Awards, where they were honored to receive the award for Best Group.

They went on to scoop up the biggest three at the American Music Awards in January of 1998. They won for Favorite Band, Favorite Album, and Favorite New Artist in the Pop/Rock category. As if that wasn't enough, at the following month's Brit Awards (their second year there), the Spices picked up a specially created award to mark the success of their worldwide record sales.

SPICE SPLIT!

IN MAY OF 1998, in the middle of their world tour, just when the Spices seemed to be at the height of their popularity, Geri decided to leave the group. Rumors of arguments within the band had been circulating since the girls fired their manager, Simon Fuller. It seemed that Geri was the one who spearheaded this decision, although the girls denied this and said instead that it was Posh Spice who was the most vocal about it. There were then rumors that Geri wanted to take over management of the band, and that the rest of the girls had rejected her.

After that storm passed, it seemed that all was well in Spice Land. The Spices were planning a world tour, including their first ever American tour. Sure, there were still arguments, but that is to be expected from five girls who spend all their time together.

Everything seemed just fine until the last week in May. The Spice Girls were in the middle of their world tour when witnesses reported that there was a huge fight at the Helsinki airport. Many people say the girls were yelling at one another in the airport, and that the fight continued on the plane and then on the ground. On Wednesday, May 27, the

Spice Girls were supposed to appear on England's national lottery show. Scary, Sporty, Posh, and Baby showed up, but Ginger didn't. The next night, the girls were scheduled to be in Oslo, Norway, in concert. Again, Geri was nowhere to be seen. The band claimed that Geri was having stomach problems and was too ill to appear. They said they wished she would get well soon. But the following Sunday, May 31, Geri's lawyers announced that she was leaving the band due to "differences" between her and the rest of the band members. Geri said, "I'm sure the group will continue to be successful, and I wish them all the best—P.S. I'll be back." The rest of the Spice Girls said they were sad about the split, but that they would continue to do what they do best—with or without Geri. Emma, Victoria, and the two Mels said they would go ahead with the American leg of the tour as a quartet. They were heard to say, "See you in the stadiums, friendship never ends!" And Mel B said, "The Spice Girls are the Spice Girls, no matter who's involved."

How did the fans feel? As usual, reactions were mixed. Some said Geri should be replaced, and some said she could never be replaced. One fan, whose favorite Spice Girl was Ginger, said, "She was always the one that kept the group alive and going. She was pretty much the spokesperson for the whole group." Another person sounded more confident: "There'll be something missing, but they'll survive it."

One thing is for sure, everyone has an opinion, even those who aren't fans. One definite non-fan said that the band would be fine if they replaced Geri with a good-looking girl who can barely sing. Ouch! It just goes to show how much the band has impacted everyone around the world. Whatever happens, all true Spice fans out there will be wishing everyone—the remaining Spice Girls and Geri—good luck!